**ALWAYS BRING YOUR
CARD WITH YOU.**

MUHAMMAD ALI

About the Book

Once, when Muhammad Ali was a little boy, his bike was taken away from him. The policeman he complained to offered to teach him how to box, so that he could defend himself. Soon the young Ali was a good boxer and began to have bouts with boys from all over the state. Not too many years later Ali became the champion of the world. Many people even said he was the greatest boxer who ever lived. Here, in easy-to-read language, is the story of the popular Muhammad Ali.

MUHAMMAD ALI

by Beth P. Wilson

illustrated by Floyd Sowell

G. P. PUTNAM'S SONS   NEW YORK

For Maryum, Reeshemah, Jamillah and Ibn
Muhammad.

Text copyright © 1974 by Beth P. Wilson
Illustrations copyright © 1974 by Floyd Sowell
All rights reserved. Published simultaneously in
Canada by Longman Canada Limited, Toronto.
SBN: GB-399-6088-5
SBN: TR-399-20398-2
Library of Congress Catalog Card Number: 73-91219

PRINTED IN THE UNITED STATES OF AMERICA
07209

MUHAMMAD ALI

Muhammad Ali was born in Louisville, Kentucky, on January 17, 1942. His parents named him Cassius Marcellus Clay. It was a big name, but Cassius was a big baby who grew fast and strong. When he was three, bus drivers thought he was five years old. People liked this brown boy. Some would say, "Looks like he'll be a prizefighter." They thought he might become another Joe Louis, a world champion who was black.

When Cassius started school, he made many friends. Often a crowd of neighbor boys would come over and sit on the Clay porch. Big as well as little boys liked to listen to Cassius, who always found something to say.

Sometimes Cassius would try to boss the older boys. But he did not like fights and would run away when trouble began.

Cassius played with his younger brother, Rudolph, too. Rudolph looked up to Cassius because he could run so fast. Cassius was always running. Every afternoon he raced his dog around the house and up and down the street. And on Sundays he ran ahead of his family when they walked to church.

The Clay family liked painting and music. They had happy times together. But now and then Mr. Clay came home angry and upset. Something had happened to remind him that black people living in the South might be treated badly at any time. Cassius' father talked about being called names and being told that his place was at the end of the line at the county fair. Cassius remembered a hot day downtown when no one would give him a drink of water because he was a black boy.

Cassius thought about all the

trouble black people had.
Sometimes at night he would lie
in bed crying. Why did some
white people act so hatefully?
And why did black people have to
suffer just for being black?

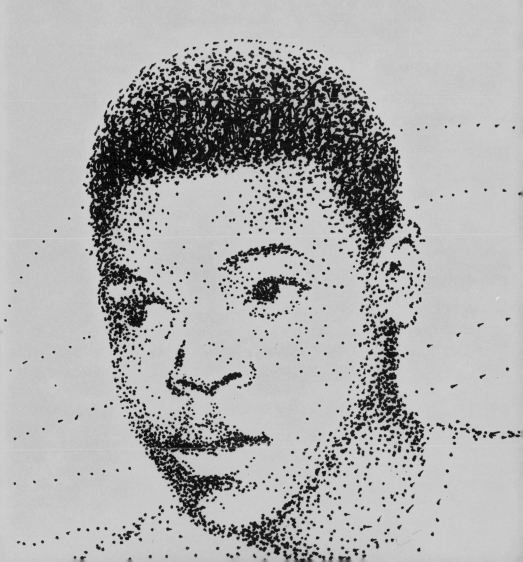

Cassius had a much easier life than many black boys. When he was twelve years old, his father, a sign painter, bought him a shiny new bicycle. He rode it all around for everyone to see.

The next day he rode his bike to a downtown department store, where some black businessmen had set up a home show. Cassius stayed to eat the free popcorn and candy. But when he started for home, he found that his bike was gone. He was so angry that he jumped up and down. Then he began to cry. A lady told him to tell the policeman downstairs.

Cassius ran up to the policeman, crying, "Somebody stole my bike. I want it back. If I find the kid who stole my bike, I'll whip him!" The policeman told Cassius that he gave boxing lessons at a gym. "If you plan to whip somebody," he said, "maybe you'd better come down and learn how."

The new bike was never found, and Cassius forgot about the policeman and the gym. Then, one day, he saw him on television, in a show called *Tomorrow's Champions*. The policeman's name was Joe Martin. Cassius could not believe his eyes! The following day he went to the gym and told Mr. Martin that he was ready to start boxing lessons.

Cassius stood four feet tall and weighed 87 pounds. He seemed like most other boys when he started. But soon Joe Martin saw that he learned fast and showed great speed. He skipped around the gym, punched bags, and did shadow boxing faster than most of the boys.

Cassius raced the school bus every morning. Then he went to the gym every day after school. His parents praised him when they saw that he really wanted to learn boxing. Later they bought him a motor scooter so he could get to the gym in a hurry.

In 1954, Cassius had his first fight on television with a white boy named Ronnie O'Keefe. They boxed three rounds in six minutes. Cassius won a split decision, with two judges scoring for him and one judge scoring against him.

In 1956, when Cassius was fourteen years old, he saw his name in the paper for the first time. He had won the light heavyweight title in the Louisville Golden Gloves tournament.

Three years later, Cassius won the national Golden Gloves light heavyweight championship in Chicago. He was seventeen, stood six feet tall, and weighed 170 pounds.

He was the best amateur boxer from Kentucky and eager to fight in the Pan American Games.

But first he boxed a southpaw, or left-handed fighter, named Amos Johnson. Johnson hit Clay's face with left jabs so many times that Clay said he never wanted to box a southpaw again. The split decision, by the judges, kept Clay out of the Pan American Games.

Now Clay wanted to win more than ever. Before he was out of high school, he met many boxers and won every fight. Some of his opponents were southpaws, too.

In June, 1960, Cassius Marcellus Clay was graduated from Central High School in Louisville. He made high marks only in gym, but this did not upset him. Most of all, he wanted to win a world boxing title. He had to do it!

Clay began to train very hard. Early each morning he ran a few miles in the city park or at the racetrack. On weekends he traveled hundreds of miles to box in tournaments. He went all around Kentucky and to nearby states. Rudy and the boxing team went with him on these trips. Sometimes Rudy acted as a sparring partner for his brother.

22

Big crowds followed Clay
wherever he went. Some people
called him a loudmouth because
he kept saying that he would win
in the Olympic Games and go on
to become world champion. But
most people liked him because he
was a friendly young man.
Children liked him, too.
Sometimes he took twenty boys
and girls for a ride in his traveling
bus and then bought them ice-
cream cones.

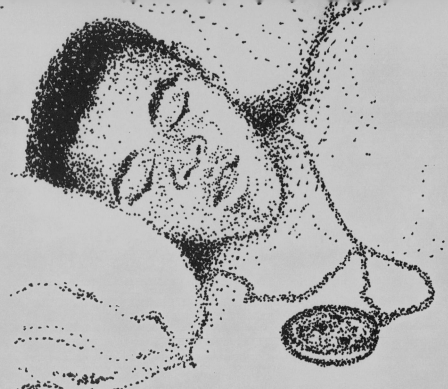

Cassius Clay lost only 7 fights
out of 130. He would be asked to
box at the 1960 Olympic Games
in Rome, Italy. The finest amateur
boxers, from all over the world,
would be there. Clay wanted to
go, but he was afraid to fly. He
hated airplanes. Friends and
business people talked to him.

They told him this was his big
chance to move up to the top.
Now Clay had to fight with
himself and see if he could win.
After thinking for a long time, he
made the trip.

On September 5, 1960, 16,000
fans sat in the beautiful Palazzo
dello Sporto to see the Olympic
boxing finals. Cassius Clay scored
his forty-fourth straight win and
became king of amateur light
heavyweights. That night he wore
his gold medal to bed. Later he
said, "I didn't sleep too good
because I had to sleep so the medal
wouldn't cut me. But I didn't care.
I was the Olympic champion."

Nearly 300 of the world's best amateur boxers stayed in the Olympic Village. Still, Clay stood out from the rest. He had his picture taken with Floyd Patterson, the world middleweight champion. And he talked to sportswriters and well-known visitors. They went away talking about this new young champion and about his speed and skill.

Cassius Clay returned to a big New York celebration. Later, in Louisville, both the mayor and the governor of Kentucky called him a great boxer and a fine young American.

Very soon, Clay became a
professional, or paid, boxer, and
everybody wanted to manage him.
"I need topnotch people," he said.
Then he chose some rich
Louisville businessmen to guide
him to the top.

Before long, Clay bought a big

car and had money in the bank.
But most of the time he found
himself shut off from his family
and his friends. He had to get up
early in the morning, go through
long workouts, and miss parties
at night. It takes most boxers ten
or twelve years to become well
known and to win enough fights to
meet the world champion.

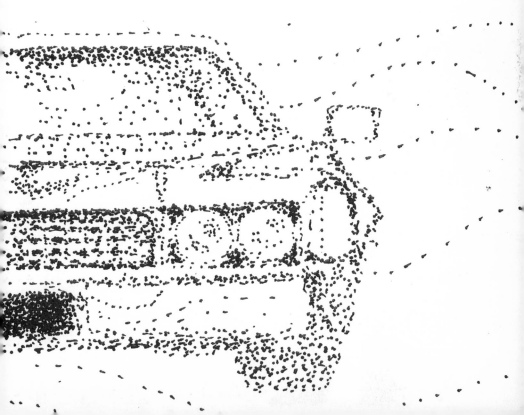

Clay said that he could not wait that long. He had to say and do things to keep himself before the public.

Clay began to say silly things before his fights. People laughed, but they went to see him box. Once he said, "I'm the greatest, the prettiest, the fastest." The crowds grew bigger and bigger. Clay won more fights and made more money. He kept saying he could "float like a butterfly, sting like a bee." Then he started to read his poetry on television:

People come from all around
To see Cassius hit the ground
Some get mad, some lose their money,
But Cassius is still as sweet as honey.

Huge crowds came to see the fights, but Cassius' poetry upset his opponents. Sometimes a boxer felt that he had lost the fight before it began, because of Clay's big talk.

Cassius Clay fought Archie Moore, Henry Cooper, the mighty Sonny Liston, Floyd Patterson, and many others. Most of the time his opponents took a beating while Clay danced around, landed long left jabs, and came out without a mark on his face.

In his first fight with Sonny Liston, the heavyweight king, Clay had a close call in the ring. Something got in his eyes, and he could hardly see Liston. He could just hold him back with his left arm. When the bell rang, he ran to his corner of the ring. Angelo Dundee, his trainer, washed his eyes. In the excitement, Clay pulled out his mouthpiece. Dundee pushed the mouthpiece back just as the referee called for Clay to come running. He was going to stop the fight, but Clay reached the middle of the ring just in time.

Clay won this fight because he trained until he became almost as speedy as lightning and because he held the mighty Liston back while he could not see to box. But he gave still another reason when his family rushed up to congratulate him. He cried, "Mom, didn't I tell you I was the greatest? Here I am the champion of the world. I prayed before I went in that ring, and my prayers were answered." Only twenty professional fights and Cassius Clay had reached the top! When he faced the crowd of screaming people and asked, "Who's the greatest?" they had to say, "You are, Cassius!"

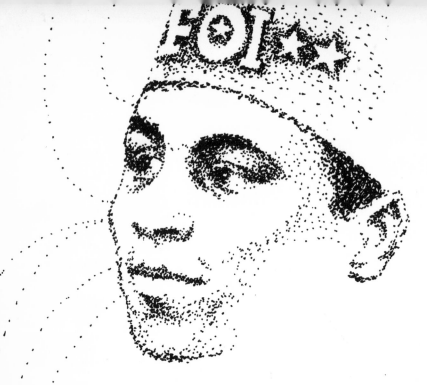

Soon people learned that
Cassius Clay had joined a different
religion, the Nation of Islam.
Elijah Muhammad, the Black
Muslim leader, gave Clay a new
name, Muhammad Ali, which
means "worthy of all praise." The
Muslims have their own schools
and churches. And the men look
up to their black women. They

lead a simple life and stay to themselves.

Muhammad Ali said he did not hate white people, only the things they did. "I would be nowhere today without the white man's money," he said. He knew that many white people wanted to do the fair thing and were kind to everybody. But many more made trouble for black people. Ali said, "Here I am, the heavyweight champion of the world. I have brought honor to my country, and I can't get a cup of coffee in downtown Louisville because I'm black." His trouble with white people in the South made him feel that he would be happy with the Black Muslims.

Muhammad Ali admired Elijah Muhammad, who lived in Chicago, Illinois. As a Muslim, Ali did not smoke or take strong drink. And he did not go to movies or dances. He ate only Muslim foods, mostly beans and carrots, and no pork. And he did not believe he should join an army or fight in wars.

Many people did not understand Ali's new religion. Some sportswriters and boxing men did not like what he had done. They said it was wrong for Ali to keep himself apart from white people. They said he should fight in his country's wars. Suddenly the World Boxing Association took Ali's title away. Some boxing commissions did not think this was fair to Ali. They said a fight is won or lost in the ring, and Ali had won the world heavyweight championship. He was a clean boxer, and his religion had nothing to do with the title.

While the talk went on, Ali and his training team traveled to Europe and to Africa. Large, friendly crowds met the champion wherever he went. And many honors were given to him. Muhammad Ali knew that he was still king of the ring.

When Ali returned home to the United States, he found the fans clamoring for a fight. Thousands wanted Ali to fight and win because they felt he should not be punished for his religion. Many other people wanted to see him fight and lose. Muhammad Ali had to fight. The people wanted him.

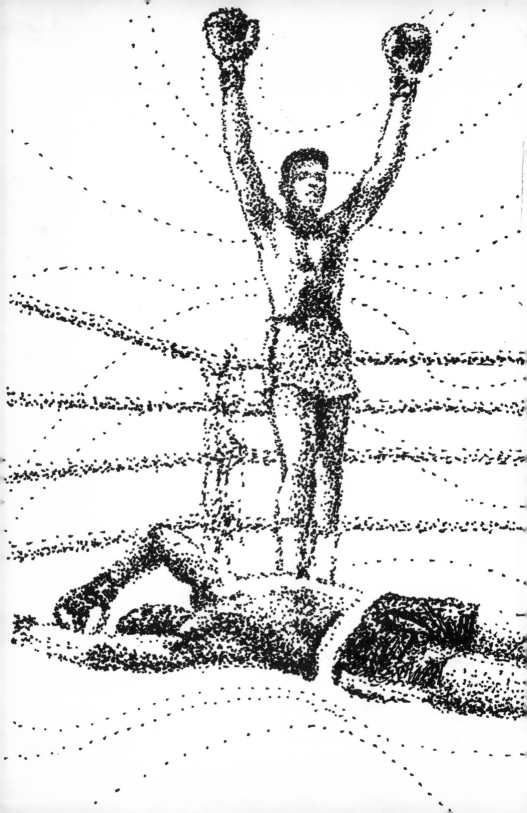

In 1965, in Lewiston, Maine, Ali fought Sonny Liston again. This time Ali danced around the ring and knocked the mighty Liston out in the first round.

In 1966, Muhammad Ali had matches in England, Canada, and Germany. He fought all boxers who had enough points to meet him in the ring. He predicted the round when he would win. And he won every fight. Then he returned home to the United States for three more bouts.

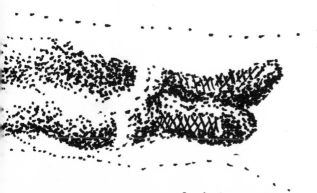

In April, 1967, when Ali refused to go to war, he faced five years in prison. The court said that he could not fight anywhere until October, 1970. His lawyers went to court many times. They said that Muhammad Ali could not go to war because of his religion. He should be treated the same as other young men who did not believe in the war. Still, his lawyers did not win the case.

Muhammad Ali suffered for more than three years because he could not have a boxing match. He spent more than $3,000,000 on his case in court. But he stayed with his religion. "I was tested for three years and I was almost broke," he said. "Now everybody is with me, white and black."

On March 8, 1971, in New York, Muhammad Ali met Joe Frazier, another strong black boxer. Because Ali's trouble with the court was not over, the Boxing Commission was calling Frazier the champion. Both men had been professional boxers for six years. And each one was a match for the other. Frazier was twenty-seven years old, stood five feet eleven, and weighed 200 pounds. Ali was twenty-nine years old, stood six feet three, and weighed 215.

New York City hummed with excitement. Huge crowds came to see Ali and Frazier box. And millions of people, all over the world, watched the fight on TV.

Ali and Frazier went round after
round, punching each other with
left and right jabs. Their faces
became marked and swollen.
In the fifteenth round, Frazier
knocked Ali down and became the
Heavyweight King. Ali put up
a good, long fight after being out

of the ring for more than three years.
But he did not win. People asked,
"How could the greatest boxer
be defeated?" Angelo Dundee,
his trainer, said that Ali spent
more time with his religion now,
but he was still the best boxer.

In June, 1971, the Supreme
Court of the United States said it
thought Ali really believed in his
religion. They said he did not face
prison any longer. The court also
said that the world heavyweight
championship title had belonged
to him all the time. When Ali
and his family heard the good
news, he said, "They did what
they thought was right, and I did
what I thought was right."

On July 26, 1971, Muhammad Ali boxed Jimmy Ellis in Houston, Texas. Jimmy Ellis was Ali's sparring partner for a long time, and he knew how Ali boxed. But Ali punched with great speed and skill, and he jabbed in a new way.

Dancing around on his toes, he beat Ellis against the ropes and won the fight in the twelfth round.

Soon Ali asked for a rematch with Joe Frazier. Then he fought other boxers so he would be in good shape for the big fight. He had to regain his title as heavyweight boxing champion of the world.

Late in 1971 Muhammad Ali visited Mecca, the holy city of Islam. This is something he had dreamed of doing for a long time. While there, a Saudi Arabian leader hailed Ali as "Fakhr al Islam" which means "pride of Islam."

Returning home to the United States, Ali told boys to study hard and ready themselves for business or a profession. Then they could help society and have a good life. He said a boxer's life is hard and uncertain, even when he reaches the top. If a boy finds that he is interested in boxing more than anything else, he should try to become a manager and handle the business part of it.

In 1972, Ali had bouts with several boxers. He won all fights.

In February, 1973, Ali won a 12-round boxing match with Joe Bugner, the heavyweight champion from Europe. In April, he fought Ken Norton, a younger fighter from California. One of Norton's blows broke Ali's jaw, and Norton won the fight to the surprise of nearly everyone. Ali still wanted to fight Joe Frazier again. But early in 1973, Joe Frazier, the champion, lost his title to another young black boxer, George Foreman. In September, 1973, Ali had a rematch with Ken Norton and won after a long, hard fight. This evened their score.

Ali said he would be ready to hang up his boxing gloves after a new fight with Frazier. When Ali does retire from boxing, his wife, Belinda, will be very happy. He will have more time with their children, Maryum, Reeshemah, Jamillah, and Ibn Muhammad. Ali and his family will visit young people in cities around the country. And Ali will remind them of his promise —"I will always walk tall, walk straight, lead a clean life, and stay with my people."

Because he stood for what he believed in, millions of people around the world will always remember Muhammad Ali, not only as a man of great courage but as the greatest boxer.

KEY WORDS

amateur	graduated	predict
bicycle	gym	prizefighter
box-er-ing	heavyweight	professional
businessman	jab	punch
celebration	judge	religion
champion	lesson	southpaw
congratulate	loudmouth	suffer
crowd	neighbor	television
decision	Olympic Games	title
department store	opponent	tournament
glove	policeman	weighed

The Author

BETH P. WILSON was born in Tacoma, Washington, where she was graduated from the University of Puget Sound. She has been a teacher and is presently an educational consultant in the field of human relations. Mrs. Wilson and her husband live in Berkeley, California. She previously wrote a *See and Read Biography* of Martin Luther King, Jr. for Putnam.

The Artist

FLOYD SOWELL has demonstrated his artistic talents in a variety of fields, among them industrial art, book and magazine illustrating, and fine art. His previous book for Putnam was *Martin Luther King, Jr.* Mr. Sowell has a studio in New York City.